MENTAL FITNESS: A GUIDE TO EMOTIONAL HEALTH

Merrill F. Raber, M.S.W., Ph.D.

and

George Dyck, M.D.

CRISP PUBLICATIONS, INC.
Los Altos, California

MENTAL FITNESS:
A GUIDE TO
EMOTIONAL HEALTH

CREDITS
Editor: **Michael Crisp**
Designer: **Carol Harris**
Typesetting: **Interface Studio**
Cover Design: **Carol Harris**

Copyright © 1987 by Crisp Publications, Inc.
Printed in the United States of America

Library of Congress Catalog Card Number 86-70064
Raber, Merrill F. and Dyck, George
Mental Fitness: A Guide To Emotional Health
ISBN 0-931961-15-7

PREFACE

During the past decade considerable attention has been devoted to the importance of good physical health. The result has been impressive. Large numbers of people now exercise regularly, watch their diets, and take other preventative health measures.

This book was developed to focus similar attention on the topic of mental health. Because many of the principles presented in this brief book can be developed and practiced like a thoughtful exercise program or diet, we have chosen to title the book MENTAL FITNESS: A GUIDE TO EMOTIONAL HEALTH.

The pressures of life are many, and it is important to remember that everyone experiences some stress. This is normal and can be useful. MENTAL FITNESS will focus on finding the level of stress that may be useful for you; and teach you ways to recognize and avoid stress beyond that level. Other topics will help the reader understand the basic ingredients of good mental health; improve self-awareness and self-image; and clarify the link between physical wellness and emotional wellness.

One reading will simply point you in the right direction. Completing the various exercises and activities can be a significant step toward self-awareness and growth in the challenging arena of your emotional health.

Good luck!

Merrill F. Raber, M.S.W., Ph.D.   George Dyck, M.D.

VOLUNTARY
CONTRACT*

I, _____ , hereby agree to
(Your name)

meet with the individual designated below within thirty days

to discuss my progress toward incorporating the basic

ingredients for good mental health presented in this

program. The purpose of this session will be to *review*

areas of strength and establish action steps for

areas where improvement may still be required.

_____
Signature

I agree to meet with the above individual on

_____
Month   *Date*   *Time*

at the following location.

_____

_____
Signature

*This agreement can be initiated either by you or anyone
whose judgement you respect. Its purpose is to motivate you
to incorporate important mental health principles into your
daily activities.

ABOUT THIS BOOK

MENTAL FITNESS: A GUIDE TO EMOTIONAL HEALTH is not like most books. It has a unique ''self-paced'' format that encourages a reader to become personally involved. Designed to be ''read with a pencil'', there are an abundance of exercises, activities, assessments and cases that invite participation.

The objective of MENTAL FITNESS is to help a person develop a personal action plan to improve the quality of his or her emotional health; and then make any required behavioral changes to apply concepts presented in this book to that person's unique situation.

MENTAL FITNESS (and the other self-improvement books listed on page 65) can be used effectively in a number of ways. Here are some possibilities:

— Individual Study. Because the book is self-instructional, all that is needed is a quiet place, some time and a pencil. Completing the activities and exercises, should provide not only valuable feedback, but also practical ideas about steps for self-improvement.

— Workshops and Seminars. This book is ideal for pre-assigned reading prior to a workshop or seminar. With the basics in hand, the quality of participation should improve. More time can be spent on concept extensions and applications during the program. The book is also effective when distributed at the beginning of a session.

— Remote Location Training. Copies can be sent to those not able to attend ''home office'' training sessions.

— Informal Study Groups. Thanks to the format, brevity and low cost, this book is ideal for ''brown-bag'' or other informal group sessions.

There are other possibilities that depend on the objectives of the user. One thing for sure, even after it has been read, this book will serve as excellent reference material which can be easily reviewed. Good luck!

CONTENTS

This book will cover four major points, somewhat like four bases in a baseball game. On the opposite page the four bases are described, i.e.,

Understanding Mental Health (first base)
Understanding Stress (second base)
Understanding Self and Others (third base)
Maintaining Mental Fitness (home plate).

You do not have to be a baseball fan to apply the concepts presented.

NOT EVERYONE HITS A HOME RUN THE FIRST TIME AT BAT!

Team work is important for good mental health. In this case, the "team" is usually made up of family and friends who can provide support and understanding. Developing and maintaining open communication with family and friends is essential to good mental health.

COVERING THE BASES TO ACHIEVE MENTAL FITNESS

Be Your Own Coach

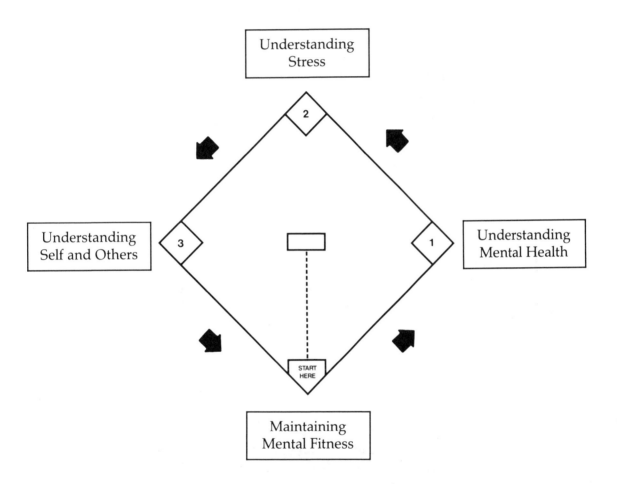

Poor mental health cannot be as easily treated as some physical diseases that can be corrected with medication or a change in diet.

SECTION I

UNDERSTANDING MENTAL HEALTH

In its simplest form, mental health is the capacity to work (be productive), to love (have friends), and to play (renew one's self) with relative freedom from internal stress and without causing stress to others.

In another sense, mental health is the capacity to cope with all of life, including its joys and sorrows.

Do you consider yourself a mentally healthy person?

Is your mental health superior or inferior to your physical health?

MENTAL HEALTH INGREDIENTS

BASIC INGREDIENTS FOR GOOD MENTAL HEALTH

To understand mental health, it is important to recognize some of the concepts related to emotional maturity. Below are criteria that describe an emotionally mature person. Check those statements you feel are like you.

An emotionally mature person. . .

_____ 1. Can fully experience the entire range of human emotions.

_____ 2. Is able to develop and maintain satisfying relationships with others.

_____ 3. Sees life as a learning experience that can bring rewards from experience.

_____ 4. Is free from debilitating fears that unduly restrict risk taking in life.

_____ 5. Can accept unchangeable reality and make the most of the situation.

_____ 6. Can accept him/herself in a realistic way.

_____ 7. Is relatively free from prejudice, and able to accept differences in others.

_____ 8. Is non-blaming of others and is willing to assume personal responsibility.

_____ 9. Is able to accept emotional support *from* others as well as appropriately express feelings that give support *to* others.

_____ 10. Can rebound from life's crises without prolonged feelings of stress, grief or guilt.

If you were able to check five or more items, you are on your way to emotional maturity. None of us ever achieves total maturity, so don't be discouraged if you did not check all ten statements. Understand that life is an opportunity to learn and grow.

EMOTIONS AND YOU

Fear, anger, joy,
grief, jealousy, love,
anxiety, and depression
are common human emotions.

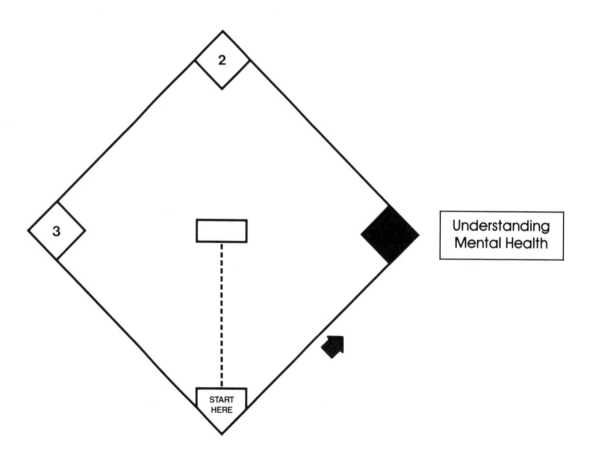

Understanding
Mental Health

You get to first base
when you learn to express
these emotions appropriately.

MENTAL HEALTH AND EMOTIONS

To a great degree, mental health is related to how well you manage your emotions. This includes both feeling good about yourself as well as feeling good about interactions with your family, friends, colleagues, and co-workers. The ability to experience and express emotions is uniquely human. Our emotional make-up is that part of us that contributes to the elation of great joy or the depths of profound sorrow. Emotional adjustment also contributes to maintaining an evenness through the ups and downs of life without the demands of experiencing continual extreme highs and/or lows. Emotions also warn us of danger and give us a way to express and receive love and affection, as well as anger and sorrow.

Most of us know that when we get physically sick it is usually best to visit a medical doctor. This person can prescribe treatment that usually alleviates the problem. Thus, physical illness has a fairly direct relationship between symptom and cure. The world of emotions is far more complex. For example, many of us have been taught not to show our emotions. Others somehow have learned that we should not even have emotions (feelings) about certain events. Males in particular have frequently received messages from parents and/or society that ''real men'' should strictly control their emotions. The assumption is that the world is better dealt with on the basis of logic rather than feelings.

Emotions are the feelings associated with all of the events and activities in our lives. For example, most people feel grief when a loved one dies. These feelings are normal and when experienced fully, they allow the mourner to adapt to the loss. If we do not know how to experience these feelings satisfactorily, despair may overtake us. Instead of healing the sense of loss, it may cause depression that can become chronic and incapacitating.

By way of another example, children who are victimized by physical and/or sexual abuse often carry the scars and stigma of such experiences into adult life. These ''scars'' affect both the capacity to express feelings to others, as well as to receive similar feelings in return. Often a layer of guilt, although unfounded, is part of the complex emotional problems that persist into adulthood.

All of us deal with our emotions either destructively or constructively. For some, bottling up of emotions may result in various physical problems. For others, the expression of emotions may be inappropriate for the time or situation and result in negative feedback.

In summary, understanding your emotions and learning how to express your feelings appropriately are signs of an emotionally mature person.

As in baseball (or any game), before a person can experience success he or she must first learn the rules and then develop some skills through practice. Practice is most effective when it focuses on the areas that need development.

On the facing page is an opportunity to review how well you understand the basic rules of mental health. Don't worry if the questions seem new or strange, or if you have difficulty with the answers. This is simply a quick way to introduce you to concepts that will be explored further in this book.

LOOKING AT MYSELF

One of the most difficult aspects of developing and maintaining mental health is being able to look at oneself objectively.

A necessary first step is a willingness to explore feelings about yourself and how you relate to others. Learning about self can be an exciting adventure or journey. Each discovery can open up new possibilities for growth. As you learn more about yourself, you may learn to realistically accept limitations; or begin to see some previously unrecognized potential.

Learning to maximize your potential, once it is discovered, is what makes life challenging and exciting.

HOW IS YOUR MENTAL HEALTH?

Everyone has a combination of emotions, attitudes, and behaviors which create a unique personality. You have considerable control over the items that make up your personality.

Below is a "pre-test" that will help you identify several key issues related to mental or emotional health. Circle the answer that best describes you. Please be as honest as possible.

My friends would agree that:

1.	I am basically a pessimistic person.	True	False
2.	I frequently wish I were somebody else or had another person's qualities.	True	False
3.	I find myself frequently angry at people.	True	False
4.	I tend to blame others for my problems.	True	False
5.	I often assume blame for other people's problems.	True	False
6.	I find it difficult to encourage and support the successes of others.	True	False
7.	It is hard for me to accept encouragement and support from friends or family.	True	False
8.	I do not have many friends.	True	False
9.	I worry constantly about things I cannot change.	True	False
10.	I am frightened about things others do not seem to be concerned about.	True	False

If you answered true to five or more statements, now is a good time to review your approach to life. This book can help you do that.

Case studies provide an opportunity to see how others cope with similar life situations. Four case studies are included in this book.

The first case study (on the facing page) discusses some of the issues we have covered thus far.

Try to anticipate the emotional implications of this case and suggest what can or should be done.

Also, try to relate all of the cases to your personal situation.

CASE STUDY #1

CASE #1
ROGER DEALS WITH A
COMMON PROBLEM

Roger is a young man who recently completed college. He selected a major he liked, and his grades were above average. By all of the usual standards he should be a happy person. As the youngest member of a high-achieving family (where all members have become successful business or professional people), Roger feels considerable pressure to succeed. Roger is also contemplating marriage to a long-time girlfriend and this has increased the pressure.

Roger sometimes feels overwhelmed about the future. Recently, he has been spending more and more time alone. His friends are starting to see him as preoccupied and moody. For the first time in his life, he finds it difficult to make decisions about the future.

Although he feels it would be difficult to discuss with friends, Roger is worried about his family's high expectations. He is uneasy that he will not measure up to the success of his brothers and sisters. Now that the college routine is over, he is unsettled about the future and the lack of structure.

Unfortunately, Roger had been conditioned to think that real men do not express their feelings. He has approached his present situation by trying not to let anybody know how he is feeling inside. In fact, much of the time he really isn't sure what he is feeling. He is spending more and more time alone.

What is likely to happen to Roger in terms of behavior and feelings if he doesn't find a way to come out of his shell?

_____

_____

_____

_____

_____

_____

(see opinion of authors on page 63)

SECTION II

UNDERSTANDING STRESS

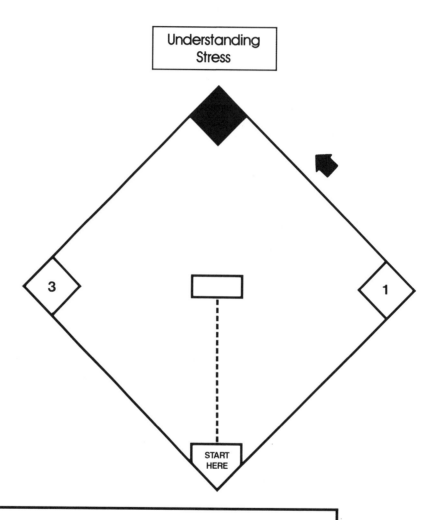

Understanding
Stress

3

1

START
HERE

Stress is a part of life. Life today is complex, and it is almost impossible to avoid stress. How much stress a person encounters and how she or he deals with it frequently has a direct connection with mental health. This section (getting to second base) will look at stress and its many interesting dimensions.

STRESS IS DETERMINED BY THE BEHOLDER

Stress is what we experience internally in response to a situation we find hard to deal with. Most of us handle routine stress readily. In other words, we are able to ''handle the situation.'' We can resolve our feelings and dissipate the tension. What is stressful for one person, however, may not be for another. In this sense, it may be counterproductive to tell someone not to worry about a situation if you do not consider the same situation as stressful. We all react to situations differently, it's part of being human.

Stress is a learning laboratory which constantly teaches us about how to successfully handle the difficulties we encounter in life. In the same way that exercising keeps our body physically fit, dealing effectively with the demands which affect our emotions keeps us mentally fit and healthy.

Anxiety is a signal that we are under stress. If this feeling keeps recurring, stress is not being dealt with effectively. For example, if you find yourself continually upset and angry, it would be worthwhile to determine the source of your anger and then find some appropriate way to deal with it. Otherwise your feelings will build and produce negative effects.

When our feelings build beyond a certain point, we begin to experience strain. If the situation we find troublesome disappears, the feeling of stress goes away. If the pressure does not let up we eventually will show signs of mental and physical exhaustion.

Stress is essentially within us even though we may perceive it as coming from outside. It is important to recognize that not everyone experiences the same circumstances as stressful.

Expected "life events" that we all encounter are often stressful. These events include the entire range of experiences: a new birth; entering school; marriage; divorce; the loss of a family member, etc.

Sudden, unexpected catastrophic events are well known causes of stress. Situations which result in us chronically feeling bad, either about ourselves or others also can result in stress.

Expressing emotions is often difficult. The ability to recognize stress, and then learn to manage it through an appropriate expression of emotions is extremely important when personally coping with stress.

People who continually hold their emotions inside, often "boil over" at inappropriate times. This may damage their relationships with others. This seems to occur most often where stress has built up over a period of time. One way to help avoid this is to talk things over before the "boiling point" is reached.

EXPRESS YOUR FEELINGS AND DEAL WITH STRESS

Expressing your feelings is perhaps the best way to relieve the pressure that we call stress. Putting your feelings into words is often the key. This is in contrast to keeping feelings bottled up. Learning how to appropriately and constructively express your feelings is a useful learning experience.

Expressing your emotions can take many forms. Below are some constructive ideas. Review this list and check those which fall within your comfort zone. Then rank in order the top five ways in which you prefer to express your feelings.

☐ Talk with your spouse or significant other

☐ Talk with a good friend

☐ Join a small sharing group

☐ Use a tape recorder to verbalize feelings

☐ Talk with a clergy person, counselor, or therapist

☐ Write letters to friends

☐ Keep a journal describing your feelings

☐ Talk with your supervisor at work

☐ Have a family discussion

☐ Exercise vigorously

_____

_____

_____

_____

Emotional stress often has a direct effect on our physical being. Consider what happens when we live with strong feelings of anger. We tend to tighten up; be "on guard," and sometimes develop headaches or stomach aches, etc.

A positive side of stress is that it can help us in times of crises. We have all heard stories of how people have been able to lift heavy objects during extreme emergencies, or run long distances when frightened. Even modest stress such as the concern about walking down a dark street at night will heighten our senses and make us more alert.

The link between continual unabated stress and physical health is clear. Too much stress over a long period of time, with no relief, can affect both our mental health and our physical health.

Learning to manage stress is the key to living with it. Finding the optimum level of stress to do a good job, without releasing negative side effects, is very important.

THE BIOLOGICAL SIDE OF STRESS

HOW STRESS AFFECTS OUR PHYSICAL SELF

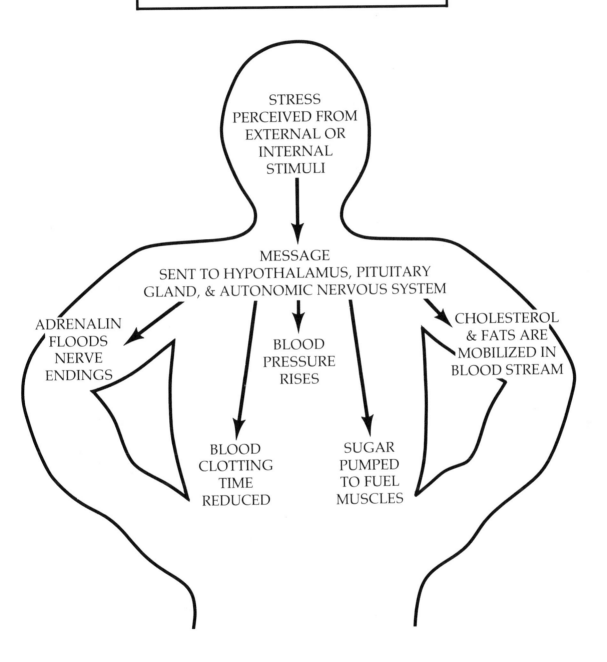

STRESS PERCEIVED FROM EXTERNAL OR INTERNAL STIMULI

MESSAGE SENT TO HYPOTHALAMUS, PITUITARY GLAND, & AUTONOMIC NERVOUS SYSTEM

ADRENALIN FLOODS NERVE ENDINGS

BLOOD PRESSURE RISES

CHOLESTEROL & FATS ARE MOBILIZED IN BLOOD STREAM

BLOOD CLOTTING TIME REDUCED

SUGAR PUMPED TO FUEL MUSCLES

Continuous stress has been shown to have a gradual damaging effect on the circulatory system; digestive tract; lungs; muscles; and/or joints. It also hastens the process of aging.

It is natural to resist or deny the presence of stress. We all have a tendency to "plunge on," working harder and harder to overcome stressful situations rather than to acknowledge the situation and "back off." For example, sometimes in a stressful work environment, a person will return to the office night after night in an effort to deal with the stress. There comes a point when the mind and the body simply become exhausted. When this happens efficiency decreases. Often taking a break (i.e., doing something else, or getting away from the work) may be the most helpful way to relieve the stress.

Learning to identify the symptoms of stress and recognize when resistance or denial is not helpful is essential. If we continue to experience stress and do nothing to alter the situation, it is likely we will develop physical problems such as exhaustion.

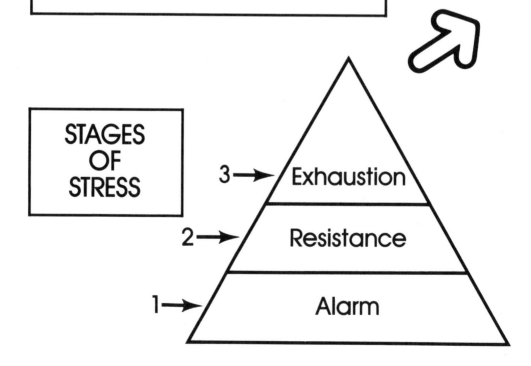

STAGES
OF
STRESS

3 → Exhaustion

2 → Resistance

1 → Alarm

UNDERSTANDING THE THREE BASIC STAGES OF STRESS

ALARM STAGE (Example - You discover that an expected promotion you had been promised and have already announced to friends is being held up for budget reasons.)

— Symptoms include:

RESTLESSNESS
ANXIETY
ANGER
DEPRESSION
FEAR

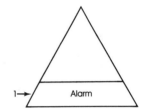

RESISTANCE STAGE (Example - You resolve not to let anyone know about your disappointment.)

— Symptoms include

DENIAL OF FEELINGS
EMOTIONAL ISOLATION
NARROWING OF INTERESTS

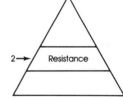

EXHAUSTION STAGE (Example - There is no change in your situation after several weeks - and you remain uncertain of whether or not you will ever receive the promotion.)

— Symptoms include

LOSS OF SELF-CONFIDENCE
POOR SLEEP HABITS
UNUSUAL AND ERRATIC BEHAVIOR
PHYSICAL PROBLEMS, such as
    - HYPERTENSION
    - PEPTIC ULCER
    - DEPRESSION
    - NERVOUS TICS

In the stages described above, the impact of stress likely can be reduced by identifying and accepting (owning) the feelings of stage one; avoiding the isolation and withdrawal of stage two; and seeking medical and/or professional counseling for stage three.

Sharing your situation with another caring person, and talking out your feelings may help give a new perspective.

Hans Selye, M.D., a foremost researcher in the field of stress described three stages of stress in several of his writings including *The Stress of Life*, revised edition, New York – McGraw-Hill, 1976.

Type A behavior has been described by researchers Friedman and Rosenman as the kind of stressful lifestyle that more likely leads to heart attacks. On the other hand recent research suggests Type A individuals may be better prepared to survive a heart attack when it does occur.

We know, however, that it is possible to modify behavior which can make a significant difference in one's risk for potential heart attacks.

Type B behavior is more relaxed and seems to produce fewer physical problems related to stress.

On the opposite page are ten statements. If you check more boxes under #1 (usually) you tend to be more like Type A. If you check more boxes under #5 (seldom) you tend to be a Type B.

ARE YOU A:

TYPE A
or
TYPE B ?

BEHAVIOR PATTERNS*

(Check the column most descriptive of your behavior)

	Usually			Seldom	
	1	2	3	4	5
1. Do you move, walk, eat rapidly?					
2. Do you feel impatience with the rate most events take place?					
3. Do you attempt to finish the sentences of persons speaking to you?					
4. Do you become irritated or even enraged when a car ahead in your lane runs at a pace you consider too slow?					
5. Do you find it uncomfortable to watch others perform tasks you know you can do faster?					
6. Do you find it difficult to be interested in others' conversations if the subject is not of special interest to you?					
7. Do you feel vaguely guilty when you do nothing for several hours or several days?					
8. Do you schedule more than is possible to accomplish in a given time span?					
9. Do you believe that whatever your success may be, it is because of your ability to get things done faster than others?					
10. Do you frequently clench your fist or bang your hand on the table to confirm your point during conversation?					

*Adapted from *Type A Behavior and Your Heart* by Meyer Friedman & Ray H. Rosenman (New York: Fawcett Crest, 1974).

Mental Fitness: A Guide to Emotional Health

Interestingly, Type B persons rise to the "top" as frequently as do Type A persons. Type B's tend to be less pressured, and often deal with others more easily. They also seem to enjoy the little things in life that add meaning.

SAFETY VALVES

Having a plan for a balanced lifestyle is important. Such a plan will take into account the need for work and play; for regular exercise; for diet control; relaxation; and building positive relationships. These items will help you reduce stress and improve your mental health.

Later in this book you will have an opportunity to develop an action plan to help you achieve a more balanced lifestyle. *

* For an excellent book on this topic order *BALANCING HOME & CAREER* on page 66.

STRESS RELEASES AND SAFETY VALVES

(Place a check in the appropriate column. Try to be completely honest.)

I do well	I'm average	Need to improve	
5	**3**	**1**	I'm succeeding at:

____ ____ ____   1. "Owning" my own stress. (not blaming others)

____ ____ ____   2. Knowing my level of optimum stress. (the level of stress that allows you to do your best without becoming destructive)

____ ____ ____   3. Balancing work and play.
(scheduling time for play)

____ ____ ____   4. Loafing more. (learning to do nothing at times and feel okay about it)

____ ____ ____   5. Getting enough sleep and rest rather than ending up with what is left over at the end of the day. (scheduling adequate sleep)

____ ____ ____   6. Refusing to take on more than I can handle. (learning to say no)

____ ____ ____   7. Working off tension.
(hard physical effort on a regular basis)

____ ____ ____   8. Setting realistic goals. (goals that can be achieved within a reasonable time frame)

____ ____ ____   9. Practicing relaxation. (meditating with music or biofeedback)

____ ____ ____ 10. Slowing down. (taking pleasure in every moment rather than rushing through life)

____ ____ ____ 11. Putting emphasis on *being* rather than *doing*. (being a person others like to be around is more important than "doing" many activities)

I do well	I'm average	Need to improve
5	**3**	**1**

—— —— —— 12. Managing my time, including planning for time alone. (setting priorities and doing those things that are most important)

—— —— —— 13. Planning regular recreation. (recreation is a complete change of pace and something that is fun to do)

—— —— —— 14. Having a physical fitness program. (having a specific plan for strenuous exercise)

—— —— —— 15. Avoiding too much caffeine. (limiting coffee and cola drinks)

—— —— —— 16. Emphasizing good nutrition in diet. (learning about nutrition and avoiding junk foods)

—— —— —— 17. Avoiding alcohol or other chemicals to deal with pressure. (dependency on alcohol or drugs deals with symptoms rather than the problem)

—— —— —— 18. Avoiding emotional "overload." (taking on problems of others when you are under stress is destructive)

—— —— —— 19. Selecting emotional "investments" more carefully. (of things we can get involved with that call for emotional involvement, it is necessary to choose carefully)

—— —— —— 20. Giving and accepting positive "strokes." (being able to express positive things to others and receive positive comments in return is an achievement)

—— —— —— 21. Talking out troubles and getting professional help if needed. (being willing to seek help is a sign of strength rather than weakness)

—— —— —— **TOTALS**

SCORE YOURSELF ⟶

SCORE YOURSELF

If you scored between 21 and 50, there are several areas you need to develop to better release your stress. It might be a good idea to discuss some of your answers with a counselor or close friend.

If you scored between 51 and 75, you have discovered a variety of ways to deal effectively with stress. Make a note of those items you checked ''need to improve'' and work on strategies to help you move to the ''I'm Average'' box.

If your score was 75 or greater — congratulations. You apparently have found some excellent ways to deal with frustration and the complexities of life. Stay alert to protect the valuable skills you have acquired.

REVIEW THIS BOOK LATER AND RATE YOURSELF AGAIN.

CASE STUDY #2

After reading the case on the facing page, make an assessment of the situation – and recommend some "safety valves" for Mary.

CASE STUDY #2
MARIA COPES WITH STRESS

Maria is a divorcee who is raising two young children while also working full time. Her position is legal secretary in a well known law firm. Following her divorce, Maria went back to school to acquire skills for a job that would pay enough to support herself and her children.

Maria's daily routine seems increasingly overwhelming. She gets up at 5:30 a.m. to prepare breakfast, make lunches and do laundry so clean clothes are available for the family. At 7:30 she drops Jose, age 2, at the babysitter and takes daughter Carla, age 7, to school. (Carla's school is 10 miles in the opposite direction from where Maria works.)

At work Maria is expected to be on time and deliver high quality output. Yet when there are even simple problems with the children, it is difficult for her to get to work on time. And when they are sick Maria feels the need to take time off. Her boss is very demanding, and when he is under pressure, he expects her to work overtime or take work home.

To compound things, Maria has been taking an advanced course in word processing two nights a week so she will be prepared to improve her financial position as the children get older. The course work adds to her stress.

In summary, Maria's day is filled with stress from morning until she goes to bed at night. She has little time for herself, and doesn't see much hope for change in the next several years.

What is likely to happen if nothing changes this picture? What ''safety valves'' would you suggest?

_____

_____

_____

_____

_____

_____

(see opinion of authors on page 63)

SECTION III

UNDERSTANDING SELF AND OTHERS

As humans, we all face problems. Understanding yourself and the things that trouble you most is an important step in solving your life's problems.

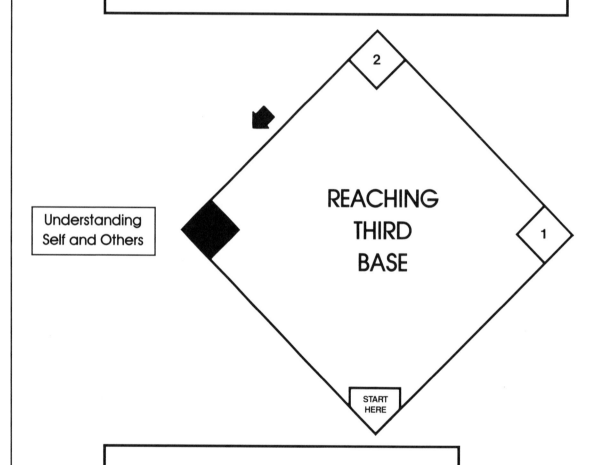

Understanding Self and Others

REACHING THIRD BASE

2

1

START HERE

Our mental health is often determined by the way we work and relate to others.

The more a person isolates him/herself, the more difficult it is to enjoy good mental health.

RELATING TO OTHERS

The purpose of this scale is to assess your style of relating to others. Be honest.

Others would say that I:

	Usually	Occasionally	Seldom
1. Communicate easily and clearly with people.			
2. Am a good listener.			
3. Am assertive in my communication without being critical or negative.			
4. Have considerable self-confidence when relating to others.			
5. Am willing to discuss feelings with others.			
6. Am able to face conflict and handle antagonism.			
7. Can resolve interpersonal problems between myself and others.			
8. Am able to accept expressions of warmth from friends.			
9. Trust other people.			
10. Will often constructively influence peers.			
11. Can assume responsibility for any difficulties with others.			
12. Am open minded when discussing important issues.			
13. Encourage feedback from others about my behavior.			
14. Am relatively free of prejudice.			
15. Am open and easy to get to know.			

If you answered "usually" to ten of the above, you appear to have good relationships with others. If you answered "occasionally" to five or more, it may be an indication you need to focus more on this area. If you answered "seldom" to any question — this is an excellent place to begin working on some self-improvement.

ACCEPTING MYSELF AS A UNIQUE PERSON

In this competitive world there is often pressure to "be like somebody else." We may have grown up with the feeling we are not acceptable the way we are. If prolonged, these feelings can develop into a poor self-image.

Learning to accept oneself as is, and making the most of that self, is an important step toward good mental health.

When you identify your uniqueness and are willing to enhance or modify your good qualities, you are on the right track.

UNIQUENESS EXERCISE AHEAD

I AM UNIQUE

To help you identify your unique qualities; there are three blocks below. In the first block list the names of people you see being similar to you and make a note of the similarities. In block #2 list those you see as being different and state in what ways they are different. Finally, identify three characteristics that are uniquely you (block #3) and briefly describe how each characteristic is or can be an asset to your future development.

#1 SIMILAR

1. _____
   name   ways similar

2. _____

3. _____

#2 DIFFERENT

1. _____
   name   ways different

2. _____

3. _____

#3 UNIQUELY ME

1. _____
   characteristic   why an asset

2. _____

3. _____

In what ways can my uniqueness become an asset?

_____

_____

_____

False assumptions about individuals can produce unrealistic expectations. Sorting out what is realistic and unrealistic is an important part of growth. For example, some people are more sensitive than others and become depressed if there is any criticism or indication they are not appreciated by everyone. This is an example of a false assumption that can lead to emotional stress. In reality, if a person is making a contribution of any kind not everyone will appreciate that contribution equally.

RECOGNIZING FALSE ASSUMPTIONS

UNREALISTIC EXPECTATIONS

Ten false assumptions that work against understanding myself and my relationships with others:

1. That it is possible for everybody to like me.

2. That I must be competent and adequate all of the time.

3. That other people are bad if they do not share my same values.

4. That "all is lost" when I get treated unfairly or experience rejection.

5. That I cannot control or change my feelings.

6. That unless everything is structured and understandable, there is reason to be fearful or anxious.

7. That problems of the past that have influenced my life must continue to determine my feelings and behavior.

8. That it is easier to avoid problems than to accept them and begin working toward a solution.

9. That life should be better than it is.

10. That health and happiness can be realized by waiting for somebody else to make something happen.

Do any of these sound familiar? Write in the space provided, a brief statement about any of the ten that have caused you the most difficulty.

_____

_____

_____

_____

_____

We have more strengths than we often realize. Others may see strengths in us that we minimize or do not recognize. There is also a tendency for some incongruity between what we feel is a strength and what we perceive others feel.

The opposite page provides space to assess your strengths as *you* see them as well as how you perceive *others* see them.

An example of someone who underestimates his/her strengths is a person who cannot accept praise without needing to negate it in some way. This same person is not likely to accept a challenging assignment because of an underlying fear s/he is not capable and would not do a satisfactory job.

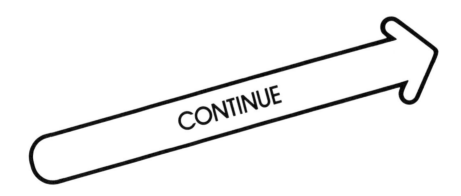

CONTINUE

ASSESSING MY STRENGTHS

Write brief statements about the following. Be realistic and honest.

1. Things I feel I do well:

_____

_____

_____

_____

_____

2. Things other people consider as my strengths:

_____

_____

_____

_____

_____

3. Things I can do for others to help them recognize and realize *their* strengths.

_____

_____

_____

_____

_____

Understanding the basic needs of others will help you understand how to better relate to them. Human relationships are developed when people give and receive freely to and from each other. Relationships that develop when only one person's needs are being met tend to be shallow and short-lived.

Knowing that others need to feel important; need to be appreciated; and need to have others interested in them, is essential to build good human relationships.

UNDERSTANDING BASIC NEEDS OF SELF AND OTHERS

UNIVERSAL HUMAN NEEDS

Human beings have many needs. When met, these needs help people stay emotionally healthy. A list is presented below. Add to this list any of your needs that are missing and then rank them in order with number one being your *most* important need.

Needs everyone has:

Rank Order

_____ The need to feel important to one's self, and in the eyes of others.

_____ The need to be perceived as successful by self and others.

_____ The need to be needed and/or wanted.

_____ The need to feel useful.

_____ The need to be loved, appreciated, accepted, and/or recognized by others.

_____ The need to feel influential.

_____ The need to belong to something bigger than self.

_____ The need to experience growth in skills or learning.

_____ The need for adventure.

Others:

_____ _____

_____ _____

_____ _____

_____ _____

Understanding and accepting yourself is the first step toward relating successfully to others!

During counseling it is not uncommon to encounter individuals who are obsessed with a distorted assumption that friends and family do not like them. A significant event in the counseling process is when these individuals become aware that it is they who do not like or accept themselves.

The underlying feelings of those who have a difficult time accepting themselves, often cause feelings of personal unworthiness to be projected to others.

THIRD BASE IS IN SIGHT!

BUILDING BETTER RELATIONSHIPS

Circle the number that best represents the way you relate to others.

I don't listen to what is really being said.	1	2	3	4	5	I listen with genuine interest.
I cut people off in conversation.	1	2	3	4	5	I let people finish before jumping in with my thoughts.
I make judgments about people before getting to know them.	1	2	3	4	5	I do not let first impressions determine a relationship.
I am not interested in other people's problems or ideas.	1	2	3	4	5	I devote attention to other person before immediately telling about myself.
I have no interest in the success of others.	1	2	3	4	5	I can honestly compliment and encourage the success of others.
I am unable to tolerate joking and kidding by others.	1	2	3	4	5	I am able to enjoy humor of all forms.
I discourage opinions which differ from my own.	1	2	3	4	5	I respond to new ideas with enthusiasm.
I show impatience with others in nonverbal ways that express diapproval.	1	2	3	4	5	My body language basically shows approval of others.

(If you have more 1's and 2's than 4's and 5's, this may be an indication you need additional work in learning to work with others.)

Frequently we get into patterns of relating that are not satisfying yet we are unable to change a pattern because it is so much a part of us.

Being aware of how we relate to family and friends is an important first step.

Recognizing we can change patterns that have brought us difficulties in the past is the second step.

On the facing page are typical patterns that lead to relationship difficulties.

INTERPERSONAL HABITS TO AVOID

Poor interpersonal habits are like old friends – they are hard to give up.

NEGATIVE PATTERNS IN INTERPERSONAL RELATIONSHIPS

Interacting with people can be either an experience that produces negative feelings, or a positive one that produces good feelings.

The ability to build warm and supportive relationships, without giving up integrity or identity is essential. Being able to say, ''I disagree with you but will explore other alternatives,'' is a healthy approach.

Following are interpersonal relationship patterns to be avoided:

1. Do not relate to others by automatically placing them in ''boxes.'' This does not allow much opportunity to get to know a person as a unique individual. For example, you may think, ''I do not like Alice because she lives in a poor part of town.'' You have put Alice in a negative box without relating to her as a person.

2. Combative styles in relationships should be avoided. Relationships often become strained when there is a tendency to be argumentative and rigid. While some people enjoy arguing, most do not. If you set up disagreements in your conversations, people will learn to avoid you rather than enter a ''contest'' of wills every time they talk with you.

3. It is equally annoying to be so agreeable you don't seem to have unique qualities. If you tend to be smiley and without an opinion, even when you disagree on a serious subject, people will discredit your willingness to speak your feelings and may begin to distrust you.

Which of the above most closely resembles you? Jot your response below, and explain your reasons. Are there any other negative patterns in your ''interpersonal style''?

_____

_____

_____

_____

_____

Becoming more aware of one's self helps to understand why relationships are sometimes difficult. Accepting responsibility for conflicts and interpersonal problems is an important first step toward positive change.

CASE STUDY #3

CASE STUDY #3
JOHN RELATES TO
FAMILY AND FRIENDS

John, age 37, is a construction worker. He and his wife, Shirley, have four children, the youngest of whom is a high school junior. John frequently has conflicts on the job and at home. He does not know why he becomes involved with other people to the point of getting into an argument. He often winds up alienating people who could be his friends. He feels upset with himself after arguing with his wife or a family member when they try to communicate with him.

John is vaguely aware he has not been promoted because of his inability to get along with his co-workers. Also, he recently was threatened with divorce by his wife after an especially intense argument. His relationship with the children, which has never been strong, has deteriorated. His family views John as extremely judgmental and critical. To avoid constant arguments, his family and friends tend to stay away from him.

John has difficulty understanding himself, and even more difficulty understanding his trouble of getting along with others. Things have reached a point where he genuinely wants help to try and correct some of his problems.

What do you think are his chances for significant change? What suggestions would you make?

_____

_____

_____

_____

_____

(For views of the authors, see page 63.)

44

SECTION IV

MAINTAINING GOOD MENTAL HEALTH

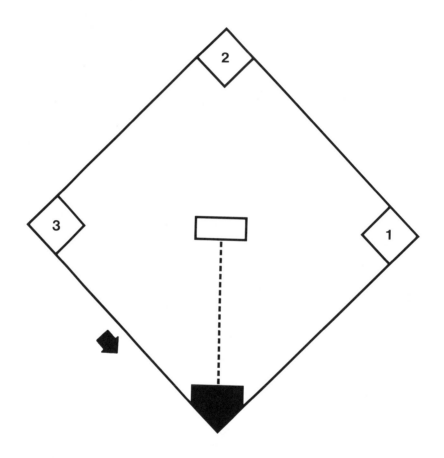

| GETTING TO HOME BASE |

NOTHING WORTHWHILE IS EASY. HOWEVER ONCE YOU BECOME MORE FIT MENTALLY IT IS IMPORTANT TO *MAINTAIN* WHAT YOU HAVE ACCOMPLISHED.

THIS SECTION OF THE BOOK WILL GIVE YOU SOME IDEAS ON HOW TO MAINTAIN IMPROVEMENTS YOU HAVE MADE IN YOUR EMOTIONAL FITNESS.

TEN STEPS FOR MAINTAINING MENTAL FITNESS

1. **Become aware of your needs.** The first step is to accept yourself. Remember, the unconscious part of your brain really knows you. When you force yourself to act differently, it will show. If your life is unduly boring — or if you feel put upon or neglected — admit it and do something about it, rather than just saying, ''This is the pits.''

2. **Let your needs be known.** Assert yourself and clearly present your feelings without attacking others. This will avoid allowing negative feelings to build up and get expressed in some negative way either internally (stress) or externally (inappropriate behavior).

3. **Demonstrate behavior that reflects high self-esteem.** This can be accomplished via body language and attitude. If you look alert and interested, and follow with a cheerful smile — others will recognize the good feelings you have about yourself.

4. **Work to improve yourself, by:**

    learning — by reading; enrolling in academic or self-improvement classes; or working with others

    challenges — do something new every few months that you have not done before that seem interesting or like fun

    physical health & appearance — improve your nutrition; get adequate rest; engage in regular exercise

    spirit — spend time with optimistic people; follow a spiritual program; work on projecting a positive attitude

5. **Stop negative value judgments about yourself and others.** Become aware of how much energy goes into ''judging'' others versus finding ''unique strengths'' in others to admire and relate to.

6. **Allow and plan for successes.** Emphasize what you do well. Build on the strengths you have and value that part of you. Remember that all successful people have regular failures but do not allow themselves to be defeated by them.

TEN STEPS (continued)

7. **Think positively.** Think about your good qualities. Give yourself credit. Keep a ''What I Like About Myself'' journal.

8. **Learn to escape when appropriate.** It is good to meet problems head on, but occasional side-stepping may be desirable at times. People often set unrealistically high standards, and become frustrated when they are not achieved. Learn to add variety to your life by planning some interesting (not especially expensive) activities. Don't wait for someone else to make your life interesting.

9. **Find ways to help others.** Refocus your attention on the needs of others. Identify ways you can give to others (i.e., volunteering for a community project, getting involved in a church program, finding a person in need of companionship, etc.). Above all, show interest in others during normal conversations.

10. **Be willing to seek help when required.** When you have problems, find people with whom you can share them. If problems seem overwhelming, it is appropriate to seek professional help. Professional help is particularly indicated if the intensity of the feelings does not go away after sharing with friends or family, or if feelings of worthlessness or low self-esteem persist.

ULTIMATELY – MAINTAINING YOUR SELF CONFIDENCE IS THE INGREDIENT REQUIRED TO PLAN FOR THE FUTURE.

TAKING *ACTION* IS THE KEY.

STARTS AND STOPS
IN BUILDING SELF-CONFIDENCE

Confidence is not automatic. It does not come because we wish to have it. It comes because we experience success. Self-confidence must be built and nurtured.

All of us experience failures. These, to a degree, can tend to destroy our confidence. If we dwell on our failures and forget our past successes, it is possible to develop a fear of the future. This in turn will inhibit the rebuilding of our self-confidence.

Another way to destroy self-confidence is to always compare ourselves to others. There is always someone more capable in an area than we are (even our areas of strength). A tendency to constantly make comparisons can unintentionally lead to a decrease in self-confidence.

If we are governed totally by the need to gain the approval of others will also make achieving self-confidence difficult. Finding our own uniqueness, and then building on it is a key ingredient to insure a good level of self-confidence.

Below is a list of ''starts'' and ''stops'' that can help you build self-confidence. Check those you feel need increased personal attention.

- [ ] 1. Start liking yourself.
- [ ] 2. Stop running yourself down.
- [ ] 3. Stop comparing yourself with others.
- [ ] 4. Start making full use of your abilities.
- [ ] 5. Start viewing mistakes as a way to learn.
- [ ] 6. Start remembering past successes.
- [ ] 7. Start becoming an ''expert'' at your present job.
- [ ] 8. Start finding areas in your life in which you can make positive changes.
- [ ] 9. Start initiating a self-improvement program.
- [ ] 10. Start *taking* action rather than just *planning* to take action.

48

PROBLEM SOLVING IS AN IMPORTANT SKILL WHEN DEALING WITH INTERPERSONAL CONFLICT. BEING AN OPEN PERSON, RATHER THAN STORING RESENTMENTS HELPS.

ON THE OPPOSITE PAGE ARE SEVERAL SUGGESTIONS FOR DEALING WITH INTERPERSONAL PROBLEMS IN AN OPEN MANNER.

DEVELOPING OPENNESS DURING PROBLEM SOLVING

CONFLICT RESOLUTION

STEPS TO ACHIEVE OPENNESS WHEN THERE IS CONFLICT

The following steps will help you learn to be more open in order to improve your relationship with others.

INTENT — Openness with others must come from a genuine desire to improve the relationship rather than win arguments. When you care about another person, openness will increase the likelihood of your being taken seriously, even when you disagree.

MUTUALITY — It is helpful to try for a shared understanding of your relationship. You need to know how the other person perceives your behavior, as well as communicate your understanding of her/his behavior.

RISK TAKING — Any effort at openness involves a degree of risk. You need to anticipate a potential loss of some self esteem. There is always the possibility of being rejected or hurt by another. On the other hand, your willingness to risk depends on the importance you place on the relationship. The important thing is that you are willing to risk letting the other person react naturally when working through interpersonal problems.

NON-COERCION — Although discussion between you and another may become emotional, it should not become a tool to get the other person to change her/his behavior. Rather, the discussion should be on clarifying the situation. The emphasis should be to determine what can be learned from the discussion that will help to build a more satisfying relationship. Behavioral changes should be determined independently by each person rather than feeling ''forced'' by another.

TIMING — Discussion should occur as close to the problem as possible so the other person will know exactly what is being discussed. Bringing up previous situations can be viewed as holding on to ''old hurts'' and maintaining them simply to strike back rather than resolve problems. Although the above makes it possible when dealing with conflict situations, there may be times when a ''cooling off'' period is necessary because the feelings are too intense for reasonable discussion.

CONGRATULATIONS!
YOU ARE ALMOST HOME!

CASE STUDY #4
CAROL LOOKS AHEAD

Carol has solved many problems dealing with stresses in her life. She has worked hard to understand herself and the way she relates to others. She has been honest about both her strengths and weaknesses. When required, she has not been reluctant to seek help from her friends. On one occasion, she sought professional help when she encountered a particularly difficult situation. Open to growth and change, Carol also feels the need of an action plan to maintain the gains she has made in the past.

Carol is very busy in her role as mother, wife, and employee. Despite the demands of home and career, she does not want to get locked into a mechanical or rigid approach to life. She feels the need for a way to manage her time more effectively and to avoid becoming overwhelmed with the demands placed on her. She feels the need for emotional support from others to cope with her busy schedule.

What ideas do you have about how Carol can develop a support system to help her in the years ahead?

_____

_____

_____

_____

_____

(See authors discussion on page 63)

(You may also want to order a copy of an excellent book titled ''Balancing Home & Career.'' For more information see page 65.)

Congratulations. You have circled the bases in good fashion. Before completing this program however, it might be a good idea to take one more quick trip around the basepaths.

REVIEWING THE GAME

REVIEW

After every baseball game it is useful to determine how the game was won or lost. In reviewing this Mental Fitness Program, it is useful to review the main points that have been made.

FIRST BASE: You got to first base when you learned to develop principles of mental health. For this to happen you learned to recognize, understand and express your emotions. People with problems communicating to others often become stranded on first base.

SECOND BASE: Understanding stress got you to second base. Stressful situations surround us. Learning ways to cope with stress, *and* manage it effectively is a step toward an improved quality of life.

THIRD BASE: Most people need help from others to reach third base. You reached third base by understanding yourself and others. By finding ways to make people contacts meaningful and productive, rather than negative and destructive, was an essential aspect of your mental fitness.

HOME PLATE: You scored when you learned of ways to maintain good mental health. Combining physical fitness along with mental fitness help make you an integrated person.

Taking action to improve your mental health requires considerable determination. This book has outlined some of the rules. If it has been beneficial, we would encourage you to review the book often as you explore further.

The following section provides some ideas about personal goal setting which you may wish to try.

GOAL SETTING IS THE KEY TO MAINTAINING POSITIVE MENTAL HEALTH.

Few people establish long-range goals. A study at a major university showed that for students 20 years following graduation, only 3 percent had established clear life goals, 10 percent had done some work in goal setting, but an amazing 87 percent had never seriously worked to establish long term personal goals.

A person's goals should relate to his/her personal life; professional life; family life; and community.

If you elect to establish personal goals, make sure they are yours – and not those that others choose for you.

Life is more meaningful when you take responsibility for yourself.

PERSONAL GOAL SETTING

Goals are significant because they provide direction for our lives. It is interesting to note that once goals have been established they tend to be met.

For a majority of people, time is spent "meandering" through life rather than focusing on those things they really want to achieve. Thoughtful goal setting can help us determine and separate out those things that are *important* as opposed to things that are simply fun or time fillers.

Personal goals should relate to both the long term (life goals) as well as the immediate future (next week).

A.   Criteria for personal goals can be outlined as follows:

   Are they Conceivable? (Can I visualize them being achieved?)

   Are they Believable? (Do they make sense or are they "off the wall?")

   Are they Achievable? (Is it realistic to assume I can accomplish this goal?)

   Are they Measurable? (Would I know if I accomplished the goal?)

B.   Goals are not appropriate when they are:

   - harmful to others

   - injurious to self

   - owned or dictated by others

C.   In order to be meaningful, goals should reach into areas where the person's potential may not be fully realized. Targets should be areas beyond ordinary achievement.

On the following pages are opportunities for you to establish some personal goals. These should be reviewed and revised on a regular basis. It is a good idea to use a pencil for this exercise.

PERSONAL GOALS

Following are objectives for various aspects of my life:

Family
Goals:

| NEXT WEEK / MONTH | _____ |

_____

_____

| NEXT YEAR | _____

_____

_____

| IN FIVE YEARS | _____

_____

_____

Career
Goals:

| NEXT WEEK / MONTH | _____ |

_____

_____

| NEXT YEAR | _____

_____

_____

| IN FIVE YEARS | _____

_____

_____

Physical
Health
Goals: | NEXT WEEK / MONTH | _____

_____

_____

| NEXT YEAR | _____

_____

_____

| IN FIVE YEARS | _____

_____

_____

Relationship
Goals: | NEXT WEEK / MONTH | _____

_____

_____

| NEXT YEAR | _____

_____

_____

| IN FIVE YEARS | _____

_____

_____

58

Community
& Civic
Goals: | NEXT WEEK / MONTH | _____

_____

_____

| NEXT YEAR | _____

_____

_____

| IN FIVE YEARS | _____

_____

_____

Other
Goals: | NEXT WEEK / MONTH | _____

_____

_____

| NEXT YEAR | _____

_____

_____

| IN FIVE YEARS | _____

_____

_____

GOALS REVIEW

Now that you have completed the Personal Goals activity, make a copy of pages 56-58 and file it away in a safe place. Then on a special day (your birthday; New Year's Day; a special anniversary, etc.) remove it from your file, find a quiet place and review what you wrote.

A day or two later, re-read MENTAL FITNESS and revise your Personal Goals in light of your current situation. Compare your new goals with those you previously wrote, and note positive changes and areas where improvement is still needed (or desired).

If you make a habit of regularly reviewing your goals (i.e., once each year); you will be in a better position to keep your life directed toward the accomplishments *you* want to achieve. This will help you maintain good mental health because it gives you a written record of your achievements and aspirations.

Good luck!

TEST YOURSELF

Satisfaction is usually present when progress is evaluated. Life allows for many opportunities to check ourselves for improvement. This progress is often referred to as "growth." Good mental health is achieved through continual growth and maturation.

The assessment on the facing page will help you measure your progress in understanding mental health and becoming mentally fit.

READING REVIEW SELF-TEST

Test yourself by checking (T-true, F-false) after each statement. Answers will be found on the next page.

1. Mental fitness is the ability to "cope" with joys and sorrows of life. _____

2. The ability to accept emotional support from others is a sign of mental health. _____

3. The expression of feelings is usually a positive step toward mental health. _____

4. We should work to eliminate all of our stress. _____

5. Stress can have a direct physical effect on us. _____

6. A denial of our feelings when we are under stress is common. _____

7. Type B personalities are persons with intense drive. _____

8. Type A personalities are more successful than Type B personalities. _____

9. Balancing one's lifestyle to include play and diet control is simply a fad not to be taken seriously. _____

10. Achieving mental health means we are able to eliminate facing tough problems in life. _____

11. Conflicts should always be avoided to maintain good mental health. _____

12. Finding somebody to be like is the best way to learn mental health. _____

13. A mentally healthy person should be expected to deal with all aspects of life competently. _____

14. The need to be appreciated is something we will outgrow. _____

15. Accepting myself may be the most important thing I can do in order for others to accept me. _____

16. Patterns of how we relate to others can be changed easily. _____

17. Putting people in "boxes" is a way of not needing to look for unique aspects of their personality. _____

18. Asserting one's self is a sign of a positive self-image. _____

19. Being "open" with another person is useful if you want to improve your relationship. _____

20. Goal setting is an important aspect in achieving mental fitness. _____

ANSWERS TO SELF-TEST

1. True   (see page 4)
2. True   (see page 5)
3. True   (see page 7)
4. False   (see page 13)
5. True   (see page 16)
6. True   (see page 18)
7. False   (see page 20)
8. False   (see page 22)
9. False   (see page 22)
10. False (see page 28)
11. False (see page 29)
12. False (see page 30)
13. False (see page 33)
14. False (see page 37)
15. True   (see page 38)
16. False (see page 40)
17. True   (see page 41)
18. True   (see page 45)
19. True   (see page 49)
20. True   (see page 55)

AUTHORS' SUGGESTED ANSWERS TO CASES

Case #1

Roger's withdrawal is an indication of his inability to cope with the pressures he feels. Because his behavior has changed, it is also an indication for concern. By not talking to anyone about his feelings, he adds to his potential for more severe stress. Helping Roger talk openly about his worries and fears of the future is vital.

Case #2

Maria needs considerable emotional support in order to cope with her present situation. It is also important for her to realize that she needs some time for herself without feeling guilty. The burdens of motherhood can become so stressful she may become susceptible to anxiety and physical illness without change in the pattern. The more Maria talks openly about her situation and the more stress ''safety valves'' she discovers, the better.

Case #3

John's problems are long-standing and one cannot assume his basic way of relating to others will change easily. The fact John wants help in dealing with his interpersonal problems is promising. Going to his boss, wife, and friends to seek feedback about his behavior pattern is a first step. Seeking outside professional help may also be useful in helping him understand some of the underlying causes of his combative way of relating.

Case #4

Having a life plan does not necessarily mean that spontaneity is lost. Rather, a plan makes it possible to direct and influence one's future rather than simply react to the current events of life. Seeking support systems through social involvement and/or civic activities, or individual or group counseling can put Carol in touch with others who are succeeding in their own search. Knowing there will be ''ups'' and ''downs'' is important in not becoming discouraged.

<u>NOTES</u>

Personal Counseling — *E. N. Chapman and Richard L. Knowdell*
Effective Performance Appraisals — *Robert B. Maddux*
Successful Negotiation — *Robert B. Maddux*
Restaurant Server's Guide — *William B. Martin*
The Fifty-Minute Supervisor — *E. N. Chapman*
Personal Performance Contracts: Your Key to Job Success — *Roger Fritz*
Quality Interviewing — *Robert B. Maddux*
Sales Training Basics — *E. N. Chapman*
Study Skills Strategies: Your Guide to Critical Thinking — *Uelaine Lengefeld*
The Fifty-Minute Find A Job Program — *E. N. Chapman*
The Fifty-Minute Career Discovery Program — *E. N. Chapman*
Balancing Home & Career — *Pam Conrad*
Team Building: An Exercise in Leadership — *Robert B. Maddux*
Quality Customer Service — *William B. Martin*
Mental Fitness: A Guide to Emotional Health — *Merrill F. Raber & George Dyck, M.D.*
Telephone Courtesy & Customer Service — *Lloyd Finch*
Personal Financial Fitness — *Allen Klosowski, CFP*
Preventing Job Burnout — *Beverly Potter, Ph.D.*
Attitude: Your Most Priceless Possession — *E. N. Chapman*
Personal Time Management — *Marion E. Haynes*
Effective Presentation Skills — *Steve Mandel*
Better Business Writing — *Susan L. Brock*
Successful Self-Management — *Paul Timm, Ph.D.*
Job Performance and Chemical Dependency — *Robert Maddux & Lynda Voorhees*

ORDER FORM (NEXT PAGE)

ORDER FORM

TO: CRISP PUBLICATIONS, INC.
95 FIRST STREET
LOS ALTOS, CA 94022

☐ YES, I would like to order at no risk* the following CPI books at prices shown, plus shipping and billing.**

Quantity	Title		Amount
_____	ATTITUDE: YOUR MOST PRICELESS POSSESSION	$6.95	_____
_____	THE FIFTY-MINUTE SUPERVISOR (REVISED)	6.95	_____
_____	SALES TRAINING BASICS (REVISED)	6.95	_____
_____	STUDY SKILLS STRATEGIES (REVISED)	6.95	_____
_____	THE FIFTY-MINUTE CAREER DISCOVERY PROGRAM	6.95	_____
_____	THE FIFTY-MINUTE FIND A JOB PROGRAM	6.95	_____
_____	RESTAURANT SERVERS GUIDE (REVISED)	6.95	_____
_____	SUCCESSFUL NEGOTIATION (REVISED)	6.95	_____
_____	EFFECTIVE PERFORMANCE APPRAISALS (REVISED)	6.95	_____
_____	TEAM BUILDING AND LEADERSHIP (REVISED)	6.95	_____
_____	PERSONAL PERFORMANCE CONTRACTS	6.95	_____
_____	BALANCING HOME & CAREER	6.95	_____
_____	QUALITY INTERVIEWING (REVISED)	6.95	_____
_____	PERSONAL COUNSELING	6.95	_____
_____	PERSONAL FINANCIAL FITNESS	7.95	_____
_____	TELEPHONE COURTESY & CUSTOMER SERVICE	6.95	_____
_____	QUALITY CUSTOMER SERVICE	6.95	_____
_____	MENTAL FITNESS: A GUIDE TO EMOTIONAL HEALTH	6.95	_____
_____	PREVENTING JOB BURNOUT	6.95	_____
_____	PERSONAL TIME MANAGEMENT	6.95	_____
_____	EFFECTIVE PRESENTATION SKILLS	6.95	_____
_____	BETTER BUSINESS WRITING	6.95	_____
_____	SUCCESSFUL SELF-MANAGEMENT	6.95	_____
_____	JOB PERFORMANCE AND CHEMICAL DEPENDENCY	6.95	_____

Postage and handling _____

California Tax _____

TOTAL AMOUNT _____

Ship To: _____

_____

(NOTE: Purchase Order number is required for billing. All other orders MUST be prepaid)

Bill To: _____

_____

☐ Send Volume Purchase Discount Information   ☐ Add my name to your mailing list

*No Risk: If for <u>any</u> reason, I am not completely satisfied, I understand the materials may be returned within 30 days for a full refund.

**$1.25 for first book, $.50 for each book thereafter.